WHY TO START NETWORK MARKETING

How to Remove Risk and Have a Better Life

KEITH SCHREITER

Why You Need To Start Network Marketing

© 2016 by Keith Schreiter

These books are available at special discounts when purchased in quantity for use as premiums, promotions, fundraising and educational use. For inquiries and details, contact the publisher.

Published by Fortune Network Publishing
PO Box 890084
Houston, TX 77289 USA
Telephone: +1 (281) 280-9800

ISBN: 1-892366-59-2
ISBN-13: 978-1-892366-59-7

CONTENTS

PREFACE

Network marketing isn't the only profession, but it certainly is a great profession. Network marketing not only offers financial freedom, but also the time to enjoy it.

I was fortunate and started network marketing in 1994, and I've never looked back. Not only did network marketing change my life, but it changed the lives of thousands of people that I introduced to it.

The secret?

Simply share the good news, "We can reduce the risk in our lives … now!"

How?

We don't have to have all our eggs in one basket. If we depend only on a job, we could take a 100% pay cut at any time. Too risky for most of us.

A simple extra income from network marketing is our insurance against this catastrophe.

Better yet, a full-time income from network marketing really lets us be care-free.

Best of all, a huge income from network marketing can change our lives in unbelievable ways. We only get one pass through life. We might as well make the journey an exciting one.

Let's get started on your story now.

—*Keith Schreiter*

UNBELIEVABLE ... BUT TRUE.

Why network marketing?

John and Mary Smith earn $80,000 a year.

Unlike most Americans, John and Mary actually spend less than they earn. Each year they spend $79,000 on the mortgage, car, and family expenses.

After a full year of work, John and Mary only have $1,000 to call their own.

Now, we come along. We show John and Mary how to earn an extra $500 a month in their part-time network marketing business.

That is an additional $6,000 a year for them.

Their extra income is now six times more!

The best part? They can learn to earn this extra $500 a month part-time. This won't interfere with their present jobs.

But, what if we helped John and Mary earned an extra $2,000 a month? That is $24,000 extra per year!

Would their lives change? I think so! Now when the boss insists on that extra project and overtime at work, Mary might consider the command optional.

Or better yet, what if we could ultimately help John and Mary earn enough money to quit their jobs? They could rescue their children from daycare, sell their alarm clock to their neighbor, and spend time with the people they love. That would be a life-changing dream come true.

Are we ready to change our lives, and maybe the lives of a few others? Let's continue.

GET PAID FOR WHAT WE ARE ALREADY DOING!

This is a part-time business choice we shouldn't refuse.

Network marketing is simply **recommending** and **promoting** what we like.

> **"Everybody does network marketing every day, but some people just don't get paid for it."**

We recommend restaurants, music, movies, places to go shopping and even places to take vacations. Recommending and promoting is in our blood. Humans are natural recommenders.

That means everybody does network marketing every day, right?

So why not give ourselves a choice we can't refuse?

Let's simply say to ourselves:

"We already do network marketing every day. We can get paid for it ... or we can continue doing it for free. The choice is up to us. And if we choose to continue doing it for free, that is okay. Charity work is good. It makes the world a better place."

And then we must decide.

* Do we collect?

* Or continue doing it for free?

Do we have to be salesmen?

No. But we do have to recommend what we like. Most adults have some natural communication skills. We convinced someone to go on a date with us, or someone to hire us at our job interview.

We just have to be ourselves, and recommend what we truly like. Have you ever recommended one of the following?

- Daycare for the children.
- A webpage.
- A restaurant with awesome food.
- A new hit movie.
- Your favorite song.
- Your favorite brand of automobile.
- A store with a "going-out-of-business" sale.
- Your children's dentist.
- Your doctor.
- An upcoming weekend festival.
- A terrific book.

Well, that is network marketing.

What is network marketed by everyone over four years of age?

A joke.

As soon as we hear a good joke, what do we do? We pass the joke along to our friends. That is networking. Everybody over four years of age hears good jokes and quickly tells the jokes to their friends. It is natural. Networking to friends. Warm-market networking.

And what happens if we hear a joke that disgusts us? We don't pass it on. That is part of networking too. We only network and recommend things we like.

Anyone can answer these questions.

Q. True or false?
Two paychecks are better than one.

A. _____

Q. True or false?
It is easier to get rich with an extra paycheck.

A. _____

So why not get paid for recommending what you like?

RESIDUAL INCOME AND RESIDUAL BILLS.

We are familiar with "residual bills." The electric bill, the gas bill, the mortgage bill, and the car payment. These bills keep on coming, month after month after month.

So what is residual income?

> **"Residual income is something you get every month before you get out of bed."**

Elvis Presley is the poster boy for residual income. His estate earns more in residual income now than when Elvis was performing.

Residual income is the opposite of residual bills. This is money that comes to us month after month after month. Residual income means we do something right one time, and then get paid for that event over and over again.

For example, we refer a customer to a company. Each month the customer buys, we get paid. It's simple, and a very good way to offset those residual bills.

Wouldn't it be nice if we received a residual check every month that paid all those residual bills?

That would mean we could spend our paycheck on ourselves!

Exciting? Yes!

Compare that to the depression many people have. Every month they work long hours away from their families. When they get their paycheck, all those bills have to be paid. There isn't any paycheck left for them.

No wonder people get depressed. They work their whole lives. All of their earnings go to others. Sad.

Network marketing helps us get ahead. More money for us, and we can get ahead of all those residual bills.

WHY NETWORK MARKETING WORKS.

This simple explanation illustrates why network marketing is the best way for companies to connect with customers.

BMW.

Imagine that we are giving a talk to 100 people. We ask them, "How many of you have seen a commercial for BMW automobiles?"

Everyone in our audience raises their hands. BMW spends a fortune on television commercials.

Then we ask, "So how many of you own a BMW automobile?" Only 3 hands go up.

Advertising doesn't have the personal connection that we have with network marketing. Advertising can give awareness, but people like to buy from the recommendations of their friends.

Which do we value more?

1. A 30-second corporate commercial on television.

2. A personal recommendation from a friend.

The answer is obvious. Yes, we see commercials for products and services every day, but we don't value those commercial impressions.

What do we value? Recommendations from people we know.

This is what makes network marketing so effective.

WHY JOBS INTERFERE WITH OUR LIVES.

It pays to be our own boss in network marketing. There is nothing worse than a boss that takes all the mental and physical life out of us. That turns our day into drudgery.

"Don't get dehydrated by your dream-sucking, vampire employer."

When we have our own business, we get excited about our business growth and our personal development. We look forward to working in our business. Life is more enjoyable when we do what we like.

What if we get a little discouraged with our progress in our network marketing business? Well, just think how people feel when they are obligated to work five or six days a week on a job they hate, helping their boss achieve his dreams.

They know they have been in the job world too long when:

- They've had the same desk for five years, but have worked for five different companies.

- They carry fresh resume copies with them to and from work.

- The "employee of the month" reward is a free coffee during break.

- The boss has no idea how to do his job, but tells the employees how to do theirs anyway.

- Everyone gets excited about the "no layoffs this month" rumor.

- They have given up on a pay raise, and will settle for a smaller pay cut this year.

- They hear about their division closing on the morning news.

- Their cubicles are smaller than their bedroom closets.

- They turn their phones off on their free days, so management won't call them in to work.

- They commute to work before dawn, and they return home when it is dark.

- Sick days are not allowed.

- They also have to do the work of their fellow employees that were let go last month.

So how do we end up in this mess of a job that we hate?

We pay for the privilege. Let's look at the best-case scenario.

Harvard tuition costs: Over $40,000 for just one year!

And that is just for tuition. This doesn't include room and board. No wonder we graduate with huge debts from our university studies.

Now, we graduate and are:

- Hundreds of thousands of dollars in debt.

- Unemployed.

- Looking for an entry position in our chosen field.

- Hoping to earn enough money for a place to live, a car, some food, and a start on life.

- Happy to give up five or six days a week for the rest of our lives, helping some corporation build its dream.

- Hoping our boss will have a kind, gentle soul, and won't make our lives totally miserable.

Now, a university education is good. But it costs a lot. Some graduates won't ever get their investments back. They may carry that debt for the rest of their lives. That is life. There are no guarantees in life.

One skeptic described getting a university education as, "Paying for school just to get a job … so that the job can pay for school." A bit cynical, but still something to think about.

There is an old joke about not having a college education. It goes like this:

"Formal education? A degree isn't everything. Our garbage man earns a big salary, doesn't have a master's or a doctorate degree, and he only works on Tuesdays."

But if we are going to get a college education, wouldn't it be nice to have a part-time network marketing business to pay for all or part of our education investment?

Because we are so far behind in debt when we start our after-university careers, it is difficult to get ahead financially. We can't find time to enjoy life or to pursue our passions.

No wonder network marketing appears as a fun alternative. We just have to learn the skills of this profession.

Luckily, it doesn't take four years and hundreds of thousands of dollars to learn network marketing skills.

Wouldn't it be worth investing some time and energy to start our own network marketing business and avoid those 40+ years of hard labor?

Hard labor?

Yes, there is a joke that goes like this:

Q. What is the reward for graduating from university?

A. Massive debt and 40 years of hard labor.

Well, that is a little grim, but it is something to ponder. How many corporate employees do we know that are still working long hours, and haven't gotten ahead financially?

Want another fun thought?

Q. Why do they call our job earnings "take-home pay?"

A. Because it is not enough money to go anywhere else.

So what if employers told the truth?

Would we take that job if our employer told us the real truth? What if during our job interview the employer said:

"Your salary will not cover all your expenses. You will fall behind a little further every month. Job security? No chance. In fact, if we fire you, you will get a 100% pay cut. Now, you have to give 50 weeks of your life to us, and you can have two weeks for yourself once a year. Or, if you are lucky enough to live in Europe, you might get a few more weeks for yourself. All of your hard-earned cash? The government is going to tax it and take part of your paycheck, simply because you work here. And just so you don't forget, there are no guarantees here. If something goes wrong, too bad for you."

No guarantees?

A possible 100% pay cut?

This isn't motivating us at all.

We want to feel safe. We want to avoid risk. We want guarantees. Is that possible in life?

No.

But if we can have an extra paycheck, we will feel a bit better about having no guarantees in life.

JOB SECURITY STINKS.

The story goes like this.

Jim's mortgage rate goes up, his electricity and gas bills are higher, gasoline prices are high, and one day he asks his boss for a raise. His boss replies:

"I'm sorry, Jim, but the economy is very tough now. Nobody is getting raises this year. However, we really appreciate the work you do."

The boss then quits work early for his afternoon golf game, leisurely leaving the parking lot in his new Mercedes.

The moral of the story:

"You can be the boss, or the employee."

The boss finally gives a compliment:

Boss to employee: "I don't know how we could get along without you, but starting Monday, we are going to try."

Not exactly what we want to hear as an employee. But wouldn't it be great to have a part-time business as a little security in case this conversation happens to us?

What if we had a part-time network marketing business that earned just half of our current salary? Wouldn't that make us feel better? More secure?

We might feel so confident with that extra part-time

income that whenever the boss asked us to do something, we might consider it as just a … **suggestion!**

We feel great when we have options. We don't have to earn a fortune in network marketing to dramatically change our lives and our happiness.

What a part-time network marketing income really means.

The salary pays the mortgage, the car payment, the taxes, food, shelter, clothing and the basic expenses of life. At the end of the month, what is left? For some people, a few dollars. For other people, nothing. And for most people, the salary didn't cover everything … so they have to use credit cards to make up the difference!

Yes, many people are going into debt, deeper and deeper every month.

So let's look at what that extra part-time income means to people with a salary.

- Now they can make the minimum payments on their credit cards.

- Now they have spending money in their pocket or purse when they go out.

- Now they can start paying down their debts.

- Now they can pay off their college loans before age 80.

- Now they can start a savings account or college fund.

- Now they can have luxury vacations and an easy lifestyle.

- Now with a salary covering their day-to-day expenses, they can start a huge investment fund and accumulate wealth, and … retire early.

Bad humor from the workplace.

Boss to employee: "Experts say humor in the workplace relieves tension in this time of downsizing. So ... knock knock."

Employee: "Who's there?"

Boss: "Not you anymore!"

Sick humor like this drives ordinary people to network marketing. There is no security when we depend on a boss or a job.

If we have jobs interfering with our lives, then it may be time to start our network marketing business.

People hate their jobs. Here's proof.

Almost 20% of the "sick days" taken by employees occur on Mondays. Amazing.

Okay, bad humor, and bad math. But we get the idea. Monday is the most dreaded day of the week. Monday is an awful way to spend 1/7th of our life. Many people get depressed on Sunday afternoon just thinking about another five days of mind-numbing, meaningless work.

So how bad can showing up for work feel?

Well, we know it is going to be a bad day when our coworkers greet us by saying, "How is the job search?" The sinking feeling begins.

We know it is going to be an even worse day when we see a completely empty parking lot when we get to work at 9:00 AM. The sinking feeling begins. We know this isn't going to end well.

IS THIS NETWORK MARKETING BUSINESS GUARANTEED?

What if something goes wrong?

What if things just don't work out the way we hope?

Can we avoid risk forever?

No. Not a chance.

Life involves risk. Even a guaranteed job for life is a myth. Think of the big companies in the past that disappeared because of bad management or technological change.

There is an old saying, "The only things guaranteed in life are death and taxes."

We can guarantee one other thing.

We can guarantee that if we don't participate in life, if we don't take some chances, then life will pass us by. We will be sitting on the sidelines watching others live their lives with meaning. We don't want to hide and hope life doesn't notice us.

Do you know what is really weird about people hiding and avoiding risk?

As much as they try to avoid risk, they can't. They take risks every day of their lives, but they don't receive any rewards for their risks.

What do I mean? Here is an example.

Going to work.

That is pretty risky. Let's see what can happen to a conservative, risk-avoiding jobholder.

- There is no guarantee that he will arrive to work safely. A car accident or car hijacking would ruin his day.

- If he arrived at work safely, his job may be gone. Thousands of jobs disappear monthly. His job could be one of those jobs.

- A co-worker may sabotage his job security and promotion chances.

- His boss could have a bad day and fire him.

- Going to work means environmental exposure. Air pollution, second-hand smoke and other risks are rampant.

Okay, going to work is pretty risky. No guarantee there, but people need a job for financial security, right?

Wrong.

The most likely guarantee we get with a job is ... **a guarantee for financial disaster.**

Most jobs pay us just enough to remain slightly behind on our bills. Jobs pay us just enough to survive, **but not enough to quit.**

It is almost impossible to retire on a regular job salary.

Think about it. After paying for the mortgage, the car, the insurance, the food, the clothing, the gasoline, the utilities, and much, much more ... is there much of a paycheck left at the end of the month?

Dayle Maloney would always say, "Most people have too much month at the end of their paycheck."

That hurts because it is so true.

Can a jobholder ever save enough money to retire? Probably not. In fact, at age 65, most jobholders add their social security check, their pension check, the interest from their savings and investments, and guess what?

Their take-home income is only 60% of what they earned when they were working! They couldn't afford to live on the 100% when they were working, so trying to live on 60% is a financial disaster.

A miracle to the rescue?

To retire, a jobholder has three imaginary miracle possibilities.

Miracle #1. The boss will give the jobholder a massive raise, an unbelievable 100% or 200% raise. Then after ten or twenty years of careful saving and investing this extra money, our jobholder can retire. Will that happen? No.

Miracle #2. The jobholder wins the lottery. Let's see, what are the odds of winning the lottery? Las Vegas advertises a 95% payout on many of their gambling games. Look at all those pretty multi-million dollar hotels and casinos in Las Vegas. These were built on the money that millions of people lost. The lottery only pays 50%. Yikes, you can't get much worse than that. I guess you can say the lottery is a tax on people who are really bad at math. If you know someone whose retirement plan is built on buying lottery tickets, don't take financial advice from that person.

Miracle #3. The jobholder gets adopted by some rich, old, and very sickly millionaires, who only have a few weeks to live. Sounds like a great Hollywood movie, but it doesn't sound like real life. The odds of this miracle? Plan on working until death.

Here are two jobholder guarantees.

1. Jobholders are guaranteed to lead stressful, underpaid lives.

When was the last time you heard a boss say this:

"Gee, you have a family, don't you? Why don't you just work here for three days a week? Then you can spend some time with your spouse and children. And by the way, I am going to increase your salary 50%. Then you will have the extra money to improve your family's quality of life."

It doesn't happen. That is why most jobs equal stress.

2. Jobholders are guaranteed financial disaster at age 65.

Their lives get worse.

They have savings accounts paying a pathetic amount of interest on their meager savings. They like the "safety" of the savings accounts. There is no risk. Their savings are safe.

They are right. There is no risk. They are guaranteed a financial beating. Their savings accounts are guaranteed losers.

Why? Because there is inflation. A 1% savings account return doesn't keep pace with inflation. Oh sure, the government says inflation is only 2% or 3%, but do we really believe that?

Look at our doctor bills or our other medical bills. Do these services only increase 3% a year? Try a one- or two-day hospital stay, and we will agree that costs have doubled in just a few short years.

Food prices? Only a 3% increase? I don't think so.

Lawyers? Don't get me started! Their fees are big, and getting bigger.

Inflation makes real buying power decrease. So a savings account is a guaranteed way to **shrink** our nest egg in value.

How about that checking account?

Is that a good deal or what?

David D'Arcangelo has an interesting view on the value of checking accounts.

First, a checking account pays no interest. We are lending our money to the bank for free.

Second, the bank charges us monthly fees for having a checking account. Let's see, we loaned the bank our money for free, and then they have the nerve to charge us a monthly fee for the privilege? Is banking a great capitalistic institution or what?

Third, this same bank will loan us money and charge us 5% to 12% interest!

Who made up these rules anyway?

It is obvious that our checking accounts are risk-free. However, they are guaranteed losers!

A jobholder's life really stinks.

Why?

A jobholder still has risks in his life ... but no rewards.

And yes, the jobholder gets guarantees. But, all of the guarantees are that he will lose.

Pretty depressing, isn't it?

So if we still must take risks in our lives, why not take a risk that can give us the rewards we want?

This makes sense to us now, but some people can't hear us. Their brains have been job-conditioned. They can't see another perspective.

SOME GOOD NEWS AND SOME BAD NEWS.

Here is the awesome good news. We are only six inches away from success!

The bad news is … those six inches are located between our ears.

We have to change our thinking. Fortunately, changing our thinking is free. We just have to want to change.

Employee-thinking is jobholder-thinking. Most of the guarantees for jobholders are bad. We take orders from someone else. We can't control our future.

Employer-thinking is to think like a business owner. As business owners, we accept that there is risk in life. We have the option of improving our income and our chances for success. We are in charge.

More about employer-thinking.

Employers are self-motivated, self-starters. Nobody tells us when to go to work, when to start marketing, when to take a vacation, and when we are allowed toilet breaks. We are in charge of our time, and our direction.

Employers think differently!

For instance, do you think Bill Gates or Richard Branson have to wait for a boss to approve a new charity project or to start a new business project? No. They take the initiative themselves.

Do you think someone tells Bill Gates or Richard Branson when to go to work, when to go to a meeting, or when to take a vacation? No. They decide this for themselves.

Another example of employer-thinking would be this:

Imagine we wanted to build a hotel in our home town.

First, we would hire an architect to draw up some plans.

Next, we would get some contractor estimates. And even though we haven't earned any money yet for our efforts, we still continue to invest money and time into our hotel project.

What is next?

Maybe we buy some property. That is a big investment. More money goes out of our pockets. And then there is zoning approval. We interview local residents and meet with the city government, hoping to get an approval on the hotel project.

Even if the project is approved, the time investment and money investment continue.

And remember, no money is coming back to us ... yet. Everything is an expense.

The construction crew starts digging the foundation. They make a tremendous hole in the earth. And then it happens.

We walk by the construction site, look deeply into the hole and say:

"Better cover up the hole. We quit. We have invested two years of time and lots of money on this project, and we haven't earned any money."

Pretty ridiculous, right?

We wouldn't quit, because we have employer-thinking. We see the big payoff in the near future. We know that if we invest our time and energy into this hotel project now, we can capture a continuous stream of money later.

This sounds a bit like network marketing. If we invest time and energy now, we may not get paid today. We might still be building our hotel.

However, once we build a solid network marketing organization, we can quit our job, cruise the world, and pursue our other dreams. Why? Because our financial needs are met from our residual monthly bonus checks.

What is employee-thinking?

Imagine we sponsor our employee-thinking friend into our networking business.

We quickly notice that our friend won't come to meetings or trainings, insisting that he get paid for every hour.

Our friend won't make a prospect list unless we sit down with him and help. And then our friend complains that he hasn't earned any money yet.

Our friend won't work his business daily. Every other event in his life is a bigger priority. Even the Tuesday night bowling league. Our friend only works to build his business … sometimes. Only when it is convenient or if he remembers.

Our friend must be reminded to order products.

Our friend will insist that we train him, buy his training materials for him, buy his product samples for him, and pay for his hotel bill at the company convention.

And worst of all, our friend will insist that he gets an hourly wage, or some sort of income for his early investment of time and money. Unlike us, our friend will live from paycheck to paycheck until age 65, and then live from Social Security paycheck to Social Security paycheck.

In other words, unless our friend changes his thinking, he is going to quit his part-time network marketing business and become another frustrated statistic.

See the difference?

Successful networkers have "employer-thinking," not "employee-thinking."

So this is our first step to success. We must invest our time into changing that critical six inches between our ears.

Our second step to success is helping others to change their thinking too. It is not anyone's fault we have "employee thinking." This is what we were taught in school. We learned how to be a good employee for somebody else.

If we really value our friends, we will spend the time and teach them employer-thinking. That way we will never hear our friends say:

"Is this program guaranteed?"

"What if something goes wrong?"

A CHANCE OF TEMPORARY FAILURE IN YOUR FUTURE?

Absolutely. There are no guarantees in life.

Jobs don't have guarantees. There will be mergers and downsizing. There will be higher-paid, experienced employees who will be removed and replaced with lower-paid trainees. Think about some of the biggest corporations from years ago that no longer exist.

Having a job is like "putting all our eggs in one basket." We certainly hope someone doesn't kick over our basket. But that happens. Many of us have friends who had their entire retirement plan in their company's stock, and the stock … went away. They went from a comfortable retirement to working part-time jobs just to cover their day-to-day expenses. Sad.

Bad things happen in jobs. Bad things happen in business.

The difference is that when we lose our jobs, we can't control if we find similar jobs or not.

But when a business failure happens, we have the option to start another business. We already have the skills, so we have the freedom to continue.

Is there a perfect combination of a job and a business? That depends on how we define perfect. I like to think that everyone who has a job would feel a lot safer if they had an income-producing business also.

Two incomes are safer than one.

We have to take a risk in life. There are no safe places. Jobs have risk. Businesses have risk. So why not start a part-time networking business to reduce our future risks? With the skills we learn, we can make our part-time business grow, and keep it growing.

Abraham Maslow said, "You will either step forward into growth or you will step back into safety."

Stepping back into safety sounds good, but is stepping back really safe?

Well, there is one guarantee most jobs can give us. If we want to be rich or want to control our own time, then a job will guarantee that won't happen.

We have to do more than sit at a job and accept what little money and time we are given.

Temporary failure advice from Mark Twain.

Mark Twain said, "We should be careful to get out of an experience only the wisdom that is in it - and stop there, lest we be like the cat that sits down on a hot stove-lid. She will never sit down on a hot stove-lid again ... and that is well ... but also she will never sit down on a cold one anymore."

Yes, not everything will work out in our jobs and businesses, but we don't want to let some temporary failures color our entire future with negativity and fear.

I think Mark Twain explains what happens to some new network marketing distributors. They approach their first prospect, get rejected, and then never approach another prospect. And they did all of this before they even started their training in their new profession.

So will every person in the universe be kind, open-minded, and eager to hear our message? Of course not. New distributors should be careful to get out of an experience only the wisdom that is in it, and stop there. In other words, a single rejection only shows us what doesn't work. It is up to us to try again, and this time, with better skills.

"When you lose, don't lose the lesson."

- I ate a bad meal once, but even though I had a bad experience, I decided to continue eating in the future.

- I ate another bad meal once (I attempted to cook), but even though the experience permanently scarred my attitude toward food, I decided to eat again.

- I saw a boring movie once, but even though I wasted my ticket money, I decided to go to other movies.

- I exercised once, and failed, but I certainly will attempt to exercise again.

- One of my friends bought a lottery ticket and lost. Yet, my friend continues to buy more tickets in the hope of eventually winning.

- One of my friends went bowling once and had a bad score. Yet, my friend continues to bowl and enjoys the Tuesday nights out with friends.

- One of my friends had a bad date once, but continues to date new people.

- We may have failed or had a bad experience in network marketing once, but we will continue until we get it right, so we can have the life we want.

See the trend?

Just because we might have one bad experience, we can still choose to take advantage of network marketing. Jobs aren't perfect. Businesses aren't perfect.

The key is that we don't let the failures of our past dictate our future. We can change and improve our results.

Will I fail?

Yes. Along our path we will have many temporary failures.

Our friend, Orjan Saele, has this story.

"Let's say that you have a one-year-old child who is just learning to walk. After the child falls, you say, 'Okay. That's it. Don't you ever try again.'

"You wouldn't say that, would you? Of course not. You would encourage the child to continue failing until the child learns to walk. The reward of walking is worth the failures."

That's a lot of failure! But then, walking becomes a habit.

So a few failures along the way while we are learning our profession aren't so bad, are they?

When we worry and focus on a single, temporary failure, this will prevent us from even trying!

What if we had a job interview that failed? Of course we would seek another job interview. Having money for food is important.

What if we had a temporary failure while learning how to do our network marketing business? Well, we wouldn't give up. We would look for a lesson in that temporary failure so that we could do better in the future.

Success doesn't come from never having failures along the way. Success comes from continuing to improve after temporary failures.

Orjan Saele has another great story to illustrate why we shouldn't give up after a temporary failure.

"So what if your first six months might be bad? Or, so what if you have some embarrassing failures when you first start your part-time network marketing business? How long did it take you to learn to talk? To learn to drive? It took a while, and there were some embarrassing failures. But now you enjoy the benefits of talking and driving. It was worth it."

Fear of a temporary failure can prevent us from trying. Temporary failures are normal in life. To be a success, we have to start now, and learn along the way.

"But I don't have time."

We all have 24 hours in a day. Thankfully, we get to choose how we use those hours.

What do we care about?

- If we care about our hunger pains, do we take time to eat? Yes, because we care.

- If we care about our spouse, do we take time to be with them? Yes, because we care.

- If we care about our fitness, do we take time to exercise? Yes, because we care.

- If we care about our personal hygiene, do we take the time to shower or bathe? Yes, because we care.

So if we really care about becoming financially free, we will make the time to build our part-time network marketing business.

Financial and time freedom will elude us if we just hope and wish. We have to make time to make our future happen.

Now, if financial and time freedoms are not important to us, we will hear ourselves saying things such as:

- "I am too busy."

- "I can't find the time."

- "Maybe later will be a better time for me to try something."

- "I can't set aside any time. I guess I will just be too busy working for others for the rest of my life."

So let's ask ourselves, "Do I really want financial freedom and time freedom in my life?"

Then, pay attention to the answer.

If our life is boring and we do the same things over and over, then we should consider this famous quote:

"The only difference between a rut and a grave is the depth."

WHY ARE MOST PEOPLE BROKE?

Here is one viewpoint that I heard recently.

If we are broke, it is probably our parents' fault.

Most people are broke because they inherited poor money skills. If their parents didn't know how to handle money, how could they teach their children to handle it?

After hearing this explanation, I thought,

"Hmmm. While this doesn't apply to everyone, it perfectly explains why many people work hard, but never get ahead."

The best thing I liked about this explanation is that it is a great way to blame somebody else for our current problems. It is the American way.

UNDERSTANDING WEALTH.

"How do I become rich?"

"It is easier to get rich if we earn more."

That is why the extra income from our part-time network marketing business can make us wealthy.

Ask ourselves, "What kind of investment program could we have if we had an extra $1,000 a month to invest?"

Our financial advisor would be thrilled to help us invest that monthly $1,000 or more into creating our wealth. We don't even have to be an expert. Financial advisors will come to us to help.

Is it hard to earn an extra $1,000 a month in our network marketing business? As in any profession, if we invest some time to learn the skills and learn how to build it correctly, then yes, it can happen. Learning how to recommend what we like and talk to others are skills not often taught in school. Once we have the basic skills of talking to people correctly, we can grow our business much more consistently.

Why not make our lives easier now by learning the skills to build our network marketing business, and then create a great investment program for our future?

What will be our biggest asset as we grow our network marketing business?

You guessed it.

The skills we learn.

You see, wealth is portable. It resides in our heads. Money, property, and other assets can be lost. But real wealth will come from the assets we will always own: the skills we master.

Success isn't working at someone else's corporation.

If we want to be rich, limiting our income to a salary or hourly pay wouldn't be a step in the right direction.

If we want more free time to live our lives like we want to, donating five or six days a week to a job for the next 40 years is not a good plan.

Are there rules or guidelines to creating wealth?

Wealth could mean time freedom or financial freedom, but the guidelines are roughly the same. Here are some starting points for us to consider.

Wealth Secret #1.

Don't ask for advice from someone who isn't rich, even if that person is a friend or a relative. Why?

Would you take dieting advice from someone who is overweight? Would you take legal advice from a criminal?

Would you take driving directions from someone who didn't know where they were going?

Of course not.

So imagine we wanted to start our own successful network marketing business. Who would we ask for advice?

* Some friends at the water cooler at work, who struggle to pay the minimum payments on their credit cards?

* A fellow employee who never started or learned how to do network marketing?

* The professional drinker and critic at the local bar?

* Our uncle who went to work for 40 years and now watches television 16 hours a day?

If we want good advice, we should look for someone with experience in where we are going.

Jim Rohn said it best. He said, "Find out what poor people read - and don't read it!" Makes sense.

That brings us to guideline #2.

Wealth Secret #2.

If we want to be rich, let's take advice from someone who is already rich. At least this person has **one** way that works.

Everyone has opinions, but we want to know proven paths to success. Sure, there are many different paths to success, and these paths have been laid down by people who went before us.

These people can give us facts, not hunches.

If we were soldiers, and needed to cross a minefield, who would we seek out for advice?

A. Someone who never crossed that minefield, but had an opinion of where we should walk?

B. Someone who has crossed that minefield before, and would ask us to follow him across that minefield again, carefully following his footsteps?

Let's take advice from the right people.

Wealth Secret #3.

Spend **less** than we earn.

Sounds simple, but a bit harder to do. We always want things, so we buy things on credit. That is rewarding ourselves before we have earned the money.

Spending more than we earn, and piling up credit card debt, is the wrong way to build wealth.

Plus, we have another problem ... bills from past purchases and monthly expenses. This makes our monthly cash flow even worse.

There are two ways to fix this problem of spending more than we earn.

A. Spend less. This takes discipline, and we can all do this with some effort. However, we can only cut our budget so far, and then we get hungry!

B. Earn more. This is a lot easier to do. An extra check from our network marketing business could make a huge difference in our finances.

Not only would we not need to cut back on our expenses, but we could have hundreds, or even thousands of dollars extra to spend and invest every month.

Wealth Secret #4.

Hang around people with more money and success than we have. They obviously know something, or can execute better than we can. Their knowledge and viewpoints can rub off on us. We start to think bigger. And we start to think more positively.

There is a saying that goes like this: "If we hang around four broke people, we are guaranteed to be broke person number five."

If you can't change the people around you, then maybe you need to get new people around you.

Yes, sometimes negative people will want to drag us down to their levels. They tell us, "Stop dreaming. Just stay where you are and wait to die."

Associating with people who know more helps us gather new knowledge and skills.

Wealth Secret #5.

Two paychecks are better than one.

We don't have to be math geniuses to see that more paychecks are better. First, use our part-time network marketing check to pay off debt. Then, use our extra check to accumulate assets while our regular job pays our bills. In time, we will have lot of assets. That's called wealth.

Wealth Secret #6.

There are three things you can do with a dollar.

A. Spend it.

B. Lend it.

C. Own something.

People who own things that increase in value are rich.

Expensive monthly car lease payments, costume jewelry, the latest fashions, and over-the-top holidays are all expenses, not assets. These things don't hold their value.

Wealth Secret #7.

Wealth resides inside of our heads.

Physical assets can be lost, but we will always have our skills and knowledge. No one can take that away.

The best leveraged investment we can make is in ourselves. Want to double our income? Simply double our skills or knowledge and our business will double.

Unfortunately, this doesn't work so well with a job. The boss controls our income no matter how much we improve.

That is why owning our own business is great. We can see immediate results, and we are not limited by a boss or company budget for our reward.

Here is a little test.

Which would you want more in your network marketing career?

A. Education and skills.

B. Money.

If we are lucky and sponsor a superstar, every night we will stay awake worrying if the company will survive, if our superstar will stay loyal, etc. We will worry because we'll know we were lucky and that it will be difficult to be that lucky again.

However, if we have the education on how to build a business, we won't have this stress in our life. We will know that we have the skills to duplicate our current success no matter what happens with our present company, our downline, the economy, etc. We can always start again and rebuild our bonus check.

So if we are lucky, and we would like to get a good night's sleep, let's take the time to learn the skills to be a successful network marketer.

Wealth Secret #8.

If we can do it small, then we can do it big.

When we look at a goal, such as becoming rich, we see the final destination. That is intimidating. We wonder, "How will I ever get there? I don't even have $100 to my name. I am broke."

This is how real people become millionaires.

First, they become a "hundred-aire."

They learn enough skills to accumulate $100.

Second, they become a "thousand-aire."

Once they know how to accumulate $100, then it is just a matter of time before they can accumulate $1,000.

Third, **then** they become a "million-aire."

That's it. When we learn how to do it small, we can then grow that seed of success and make our results bigger.

If we can't learn how to accumulate $100 after years of working on a job, how will we ever have the discipline to accumulate even $1,000?

It is easier for most people to eat out at restaurants, play video games, smoke cigarettes, buy lottery tickets, drink beer, buy non-necessities that are on sale, buy a new car on payments, etc. - than it is for them to save $100.

Until that pattern is broken, even the best network marketing opportunity won't solve their problems.

Wealth Secret #9.

One good business opportunity is better than a lifetime of work!

We all know someone who started a business, and the business grew. This person now earns more money from his business in one year than he earned in ten years of collecting a salary from a job.

We know people who bought real estate 20 or 30 years ago. When they sell their real estate assets, they will earn more money from their real estate than they would in a lifetime of working for a salary.

Pay raises from a job are very limited. Only in our own business can we earn 5, 10, or even 20 times our current income just by increasing the success of our business.

Having a business gives us the chance to ramp up our income far faster than waiting for a salary raise at work.

Wealth Secret #10.

Opportunity knocks and some people will complain about the noise. We don't want to be one of those people.

We need opportunity to change our lives and move forward. If we continue doing the same things, then our results will also be the same.

We want to look for opportunity … and engage.

WHY WE SHOULD LOVE WHAT WE DO.

Ever hear this?

"Mondays don't stink; it is your job that stinks."

If we don't enjoy our job, how long are we going to keep doing it? Until we retire? Until we get fired? Not a pleasant thought.

Let's quote comedian Drew Carey. He said,

"Oh, you hate your job? Why didn't you say so? There is a support group for that. It's called EVERYBODY, and they meet at the bar."

Sad. True for many. This is not the life we want.

Let's ask ourselves this: "How many people do we know who hate their jobs? How many people do we know who hate waking up early, leaving their families, and commuting to their terrible jobs?"

We are not alone. There are many, many other people like us who want to sleep in on Mondays, and then do what they want to do with their lives.

How are we programmed into submission?

Comedian Ellen Goodman says it best: "Normal is getting dressed in clothes that you buy for work and driving through traffic in a car that you are still paying for - in order to get to the job you need to pay for the clothes and the car, and the house you leave vacant all day so you can afford to live in it."

Groan. This happens, and we just don't notice it.

That quote is depressing and very, very true.

But, could life be different for us?

Of course. However, it won't change unless we plan to escape from our status quo. We've all heard this quote:

"If you enjoy what you do, you will never work another day in your life."

Excellent. Now that would be living the dream.

Author Seth Godin says:

"Instead of wondering when your next vacation is, maybe you should set up a life that you don't need to escape from."

Are we starting to see a trend?

Our happiness can soar simply by loving what we do.

Is a network marketing career for everyone?

No. Not everyone wants the same career. However, there are many people who want to be involved in our networking business. Do you think we are the only people to ever want more free time, more money, greater career satisfaction?

Certainly not. Many people have the same dreams and desires that we do.

Before we learn how to locate these individuals, let's get an overall picture of people that we come into contact with.

First, we must realize that not everyone wants to or should participate in network marketing. There are lots of reasons why some people shouldn't.

For example, some people enjoy their work and careers.

They are happy with the way things are. We certainly don't want to change that.

Let's say that John is a basketball coach for the local college. He loves his job. He arrives early and leaves late, but loves every minute of his day.

What does his family think? They love basketball too.

His children are active participants. His wife coaches the local high school team.

What does the family do at night? They watch basketball videos.

Where do they go on vacation? To basketball instructional camps.

If John's family won the lottery, what they would do?

Would they use the money to open a restaurant? Would they take long hikes in the mountains? Or, would they still coach basketball and watch basketball games?

You guessed it. They wouldn't change their daily routine. They love what they do. Basketball is all they ever wanted in life, and they are living their dreams.

Should John take time from his dream life to do network marketing?

Probably not.

However, there is another side to this story.

John may love basketball, but his coaching job doesn't pay him enough money to support his family and to do the other things they enjoy. Or, maybe his coaching job takes too much time away from his family.

In this case, John becomes an ideal prospect for network marketing to solve his time and money problems.

Remember, this is John's choice, not ours. It is up to John to decide if he wants to build a part-time business, and if network marketing's benefits could enhance his life.

Our job is simply to educate John about the possibilities, and then he can make the choices for himself. We are responsible for making sure John has an opportunity to make choices, but we are not responsible for the decisions John makes in his life.

Many people enjoy and love their careers and lives.

There are many teachers, coaches, farmers, bankers, fishermen, salesmen, nurses, truck drivers, and doctors who love what they do every day. If they are happy and their career gives them all the time and money they want, then they are not prospects for our network marketing business opportunity.

They are happy. Don't ruin it.

However, there are many more people who hate their careers and lives. They don't like the limited advancement opportunities. They hate the working hours, the pressures, and the duties they must perform.

They hate the time away from their families. They want more money for their time investment. They have other goals and dreams beyond their present job or career.

They want the time, money, freedom and potential of network marketing. These people are great prospects for our network marketing business.

The story of two men.

Two men are fishermen.

The first man wakes up early. By 4:00 AM, before dawn, he is on his company's fishing boat, ready for the day's work. All day long he labors as a fisherman. He works on fixing the nets, cleaning the catches as they come in, and scouting for new and better fishing locations. When evening comes, this man leaves the boat feeling tired, depressed and dejected because tomorrow will be a repeat of his grueling day. Fishing is a job, a hard job.

The second man works at the local factory. On Saturdays and Sundays he rises at 4:00 AM to go fishing.

He endures the dark, the cold, and the wind. He fishes the entire weekend. He loves to fish. In fact, all week long at the factory, all he can think about is going fishing during the weekend. Fishing is his dream, his ultimate experience.

Now, both men are fishermen.

One looks at his fishing as work, a dreadfully boring job. The second man looks at his fishing as a hobby, an enjoyable, challenging outdoor experience.

This is true of most professions. There are people who work for landscaping companies that consider gardening as work. Yet others will gladly pay for expensive tools to enjoy gardening as a relaxing hobby. Some teachers dread going to school and lecturing their students. Yet other people will beg for the opportunity to speak in public and to impart their messages.

Some people hate their construction jobs while others build garages and sheds in their free time as an enjoyable hobby.

If meeting people and recommending sounds fun to you ...

One of life's secrets is to find out what you enjoy, and make that your profession. That may be almost impossible for many people, but here is where network marketing can help.

What if you started a part-time network marketing business? Once you have built up your network marketing income to replace your salary, then maybe you can take that big step to reach your dreams.

With the security of a regular network marketing residual monthly income, a person could make a stress-free career change and not have to worry about money. That is just one of the benefits of network marketing. Of course, there are more.

When people see network marketing as the financial solution to their career happiness, they will eagerly look forward to a conversation with us.

We can tell them our network marketing story, and the rest is up to them.

IF WE CAN TELL A STORY, WE CAN DO NETWORK MARKETING!

Good storytellers make the most money in network marketing. Why?

Because good storytellers are interesting. They effectively communicate their message to prospects.

People acquire their beliefs from their experiences. If someone lives on a street where everyone works a job, that person will believe that having a job is the only option. If no one on that street does network marketing for a living, this person will probably believe that network marketing can't be a full-time income.

No experience. No belief.

Sound familiar?

Our job is to communicate that a part-time business can add value to that person's life.

The one story we must tell.

The biggest sale we have to make as a network marketer is to convince our prospects that they already do network marketing every day, but they just don't get paid for it.

Once they believe that they do network marketing every day, it is easy. We can just tell them the information about our company, our product, our compensation plan, but the decision to join has already been made.

Think about it.

If everyone you knew believed that they did network marketing every day, but they just didn't get paid for it, how hard would it be to sign them up?

It would be easy.

So all we have to do is to help them make one simple decision. We simply have to sell our prospects on changing their beliefs about network marketing.

What happens after we make this one big sale?

Once our prospects believe they do network marketing every day already, their next question is:

"How do I collect from it?"

All the resistance disappears from our prospects as they lean in and closely listen to our presentation.

How are we going to make that sale?

By telling our prospects a story.

Now, we can make up our own stories, but here are a few stories that I like to use. Use them as a guideline for your stories, if you wish.

The frequent flier miles story.

I take a flight from London to New York City. I pay $1,000 for a ticket.

You also take a flight from London to New York City.

You also pay $1,000 for your ticket.

We both arrive in New York City, but because you filled out a simple one-page form to join the airline's frequent flier program, you got some frequent flier miles and I didn't.

You and I did exactly the same thing. You got rewarded.

I didn't. You got frequent flier miles, they added up and eventually you got a free trip to Hawaii.

What if the airline told you that if you told your friends to join their frequent flier program, they would give you some extra frequent flier miles every time your friends earn some frequent flier miles?

Wow. You would tell everyone you knew.

And get this, what if you got frequent flier miles every time you flew … and you got frequent flier miles every time your friends flew … and if your friends recommended the frequent flier program to their friends, you got even more frequent flier miles every time their friends flew … and so on, wow!

This would be the frequent flier program on steroids!

Well, network marketing works the same way, except we don't give you frequent flier miles, we give you cash!

The breathing story.

Imagine that one day, the government said,

"Every person that exhales is due a tax refund. You will earn a few cents every time you exhale. And since you exhale hundreds of times every hour, this could add up to hundreds of dollars a month. All you have to do is register for your money by filling out this simple form."

If this were true, then if you saw somebody exhaling, you probably wouldn't feel bad about approaching them and saying:

"Hey, you are exhaling. Did you know you are supposed to get an extra check from the government just for exhaling?"

Of course you would feel comfortable letting people know that they could collect money for what they are already doing. Well, networking marketing is like an exhaling bonus. Everyone does network marketing every day. Everyone recommends a favorite movie/restaurant/website, so would you feel bad about approaching somebody and saying:

"Hey, you are already doing network marketing, did you know you can pick up a check for it?"

These stories create belief for our prospects.

They are also a way to help new distributors feel good about contacting their families, their friends and their coworkers.

And - these stories build our personal belief even more.

Our own belief?

Yes, a big part of successful business-building is our own belief. We must feel and believe that networking is a great opportunity for everyone.

If we don't have that strong internal belief, then we have to be a salesman, and that's hard.

Ever heard this?

"Dogs know who to bite."

Dogs know if you are friendly or a threat. Normally, dogs will lick little kids but instinctively know which adults to bite.

Our prospects also have intuition, a sixth sense, or a

feeling about us and our beliefs. So we have to manage our own beliefs carefully so that we don't sabotage our business-building efforts.

Do you want another story to support our new beliefs in network marketing?

The Social Security story.

Imagine you and I are both 85 years old. One day I come up to you and I say:

"Hey, did you get your Social Security retirement check yet?"

And you say:

"Huh?"

So I repeat the question and say:

"Did you get your Social Security retirement check in the mail this month?"

You frown and say:

"Social Security retirement check? What is that?"

I explain:

"You know about the Social Security retirement check, don't you? It is the check the government gives us every month just for being old. Once you turn 65 years old, you fill out a little form and the government sends you a retirement check every month just for being old."

You say:

"Oh no! I didn't know about it. And here I am, 85 years old, and for the last 20 years I could have been getting all that extra money. I just missed out on 240 checks of free money from the government!"

So how would you feel if that happened to you? Pretty bad. No one told you that you could have been getting those checks.

And how would you feel if I said this?

"Oh, I am sorry. I knew about these checks all the time.

"I guess I just never bothered to tell you about them over the last 20 years. I thought maybe you wouldn't be interested in getting that free money from the government."

You would be mad! Really mad!

That is why we must tell everyone we know that people do network marketing every day, but they just don't get paid for it. They don't know this, and they don't know how to collect the check.

Then, if they are interested in picking up that extra check, they can ask us for details.

We don't want one of our friends to come back to us five years, 10 years, or 20 years from now and say,

"Why didn't you tell me that I was already doing network marketing every day, but that I just wasn't getting paid for it? What kind of a friend are you to withhold that kind of information? I could have been getting extra paychecks every month!"

Now that we know network marketing is great for us, are we ready to make our decision to move forward?

MAKING A DECISION TO MOVE FORWARD.

"The best way to predict the future is to create it."

— *Peter Drucker*

Zig Ziglar once asked his audience: "Can you do something to make your life worse in the next three weeks?"

The audience said: "Yes, of course."

This was easy to visualize and accept.

Then Zig said: "Can you do something to make your life better in the next three weeks?"

Aha! Now the audience had to accept that they could.

This means that we are in control of our lives. We are not victims of circumstances. And, we should stop blaming others for our current situations.

Zig Ziglar had a great way to get this message inside of the audience's heads. Now they believed they could change their lives, and that they were responsible for the results.

So what are we thinking?

When we want to make a decision to start our network marketing business, these thoughts come to mind:

"I don't want to make a mistake."

"What if I make the wrong decision?"

"I need to think it over and delay any decision as long as possible."

"What if I fail?"

"Maybe I should just take my time thinking about this."

And we are thinking ... and thinking ... and thinking. Oh, if we could only make a decision, any decision, it would be wonderful. We could get on with our lives.

But no. That would be too easy. We insist on torturing ourselves with indecision. We don't realize that "not making a decision" is really making a decision to keep things just as they are.

For example, the train is pulling into the station. We don't know if we should board the train or not. So we think, think, think ... and soon, the train has already left the station. Our indecision actually became a decision.

We are not going to be on that train.

So if we continue to delay our decision to start, then we are effectively making a decision to keep our lives the same.

Keeping our lives the same is okay. It is just that we should be consciously making that decision.

Here are a few questions that we can ask ourselves. These questions will help us make a conscious decision on what is best for our lives.

1. What will happen if we don't start our business?

Of course the answer is: "Nothing."

Life will be the same. Tomorrow will look just like today. We will wake up early, commute to work, come back late, grab a quick meal, watch a few minutes of television and go to sleep. Yes, we will experience this routine over and over again – until we are too old to work.

Not a very pretty picture, is it? Now if we choose to leave everything the same, if we choose to avoid an opportunity, that is okay. We are consciously making our decision.

2. What do you think will happen next year if we decide not to make any changes this year? Will we be in the same position as now, but just another year older?

3. Do we think our job routine (five days a week, a few weeks of vacation every year) will ever change?

4. Are we stressing out about risking a change in our daily life? Should we just relax and continue our life as it is?

5. Is winning the lottery our retirement plan? If it is, is that a good plan?

All of these questions remind us that the pain of these problems won't go away by procrastinating on a decision.

We need to decide now.

The #1 reason for failure?

Failure to start.

We can defeat the #1 reason for failure by simply taking our first step forward.

We don't have to wait until we know how to do everything.

We just need to start. The best way to do that?

Simply contact your sponsor now, and start working together **now.**

Will we pay our success dues?

Imagine this.

There are two people, John and Mary.

John starts his network marketing business. He is lazy, doesn't get on conference calls, doesn't learn new skills, avoids talking to prospects, and seldom gives out a sample.

His "hands-on" knowledge of visiting with prospects is "zero." John just sits around and waits for that lucky break … and it comes!

The perfect prospect with the perfect connections with the perfect timing. Excellent!

And what happens to John's business?

Nothing.

John didn't have a clue what to say.

Mary starts her network marketing business. She gets on every conference call she can, learns new skills, talks to "live" prospects, and passes out samples.

She learns how to communicate with prospects. She accumulates experience.

While Mary is struggling and interacting with prospects, that perfect prospect appears!

The perfect prospect with the perfect connections with the perfect timing. Excellent!

And what happens to Mary's business?

It explodes.

Why?

Because Mary had experience. She interacted with prospects daily. Each time she passed out a sample, she learned a little bit more about dealing with people.

So when the perfect prospect appeared, Mary knew how to communicate and recommend.

The moral of this story is:

We have to pay our dues!

Ready to start our journey?

A journey of one thousand miles starts with a single step. But wouldn't it be great if our first steps were in the right direction? We don't want to travel full speed in the wrong direction.

An old saying.

It goes something like this:

"I hear, and I forget. I see, and I remember. I do, and I understand."

We can't really understand this business by reading only. We have to do it and experience it.

HOW TO TAKE OUR FIRST STEP.

The first step is our most important step. If we wait one year until we feel our circumstances are right, we will lose one year of progress in our business.

We will be so much farther ahead in one year if we start stumbling and fumbling our way forward now. We don't have to wait until we know how to do everything.

We just need to start.

Overwhelmed and want to know what to do first?

Here are four easy daily tasks to start building our future in network marketing.

1. Add one new prospect to our list daily. Meet a new person. Get in touch with someone from the past. Make a new friend on Facebook. (It is hard to get discouraged and quit when we have lots of prospects.)

2. Talk to one person about our opportunity or product. (It only takes one minute if we use the right words.) Consistent exposure ensures we will eventually meet people who want to join because the timing is right for them.

3. Do one thing to create loyalty in your business. Send a motivational article, offer to help someone, pass on a prospecting idea, or pass on a product testimonial or research report.

4. Learn more skills.

H. Jackson Browne said, "You can get by on charm for about 15 minutes. After that, you better know something." The more skills we learn, the faster our business will grow. We could read 15 minutes a day from a "Big Al" book, and over time, learn great skills to build our business fast.

All four of these easy daily tasks could be finished early in the day, and we could take the rest of the day off. Consistently doing these four tasks will move our network marketing business forward.

READY TO LEARN SOME SKILLS AND GET YOUR NETWORK MARKETING BUSINESS MOVING FORWARD?

Two things you can do immediately.

1. Go to http://www.BigAlReport.com and get the free weekly Big Al Report. Learn great things to say and do to build your business fast. Everyone can afford free things.

2. Go to http://www.BigAlBooks.com and choose a book or audio to start learning network marketing skills now. The sooner we learn, the sooner we earn.

Want a training workshop in your area?

Visit http://BigAlSeminars.com

You'll find additional Big Al products at:

http://www.FortuneNow.com

MORE BOOKS FROM
FORTUNE NETWORK PUBLISHING

The Four Color Personalities for MLM
The Secret Language for Network Marketers

Ice Breakers!
How To Get Any Prospect To Beg You For A Presentation

How To Get Instant Trust, Belief, Influence and Rapport!
13 Ways To Create Open Minds By Talking To The Subconscious Mind

First Sentences for Network Marketing
How To Quickly Get Prospects On Your Side

Big Al's MLM Sponsoring Magic
How to Build a Network Marketing Team Quickly

How To Prospect, Sell And Build Your
Network Marketing Business With Stories

26 Instant Marketing Ideas
To Build Your Network Marketing Business

How To Build Network Marketing Leaders - Volume One
Step-By-Step Creation Of MLM Professionals

How To Build Network Marketing Leaders - Volume Two
Activities And Lessons For MLM Leaders

Start SuperNetworking!
5 Simple Steps To Creating Your Own Personal Networking Group

How to Follow Up With Your Network Marketing Prospects
Turn Not Now Into Right Now!

Complete list at BigAlBooks.com

NEED MORE COPIES?

For quantity discount pricing on this book,
please call +1 (281) 280-9800.

Or email us at BigAlsOffice@gmail.com

ABOUT THE AUTHOR

Keith Schreiter has 20+ years of experience in network marketing and MLM. He is the co-author of the books,

- *51 Ways and Places to Sponsor New Distributors: Discover Hot Prospect For Your Network Marketing Business*

- *How to Follow Up With Your Network Marketing Prospects: Turn Not Now Into Right Now*

- *Start SuperNetworking! 5 Simple Steps To Creating Your Own Personal Networking Group*

Keith shows network marketers how to use simple systems to build a stable and growing business.

So, do you need more prospects? Do you need your prospects to commit instead of stalling? Want to know how to engage and keep your group active? If these are the types of skills you would like to master, you will enjoy his "how-to" style.

Keith speaks and trains in the United States, Canada, and Europe.